This book was devised and produced by
Multimedia Publications (UK) Ltd

Editor: Marilyn Inglis
Assistant Editor: Diana Vowles
Production: Arnon Orbach
Design: John Strange and Associates
Picture Research: Susan Bolsom-Morris

First published in the United States of America 1985 by
Gallery Books, an imprint of W. H. Smith Publishers Inc.,
112 Madison Avenue, New York, NY 10016

ISBN 0 8317 7466 5

Origination by Imago Publishing Ltd
Printed in Italy by Sagdos

ROME

Carol Wright

Contents

The Eternal City

Proud of its ruling past, Rome sits surrounded by reminders of two thousand years or more of former glories. The triumphal arches of the ancient Romans jostle with the palaces of the popes, and the more modern bureaucratic buildings of Rome proclaim the city as the center of the State of Italy.

Rome is a chaotic city; the traffic gives no ground to pedestrians. Its ancient stones and walls are daubed with slogans and demonstrators parade the streets and sidewalks. Hot and noisy, it lurches from one economic crisis to another, yet it remains the "Eternal City", a witness to the survival of man's creative genius throughout the ages.

Today, Rome has a population of some four million people spread over 62 000 acres (excluding the Vatican state). Romans face their modern-day problems with a certain serenity, secure in the knowledge that the city has survived centuries of crises. The Roman lifestyle – the much exaggerated *dolce vita* – of walks in the shade, lengthy lunches and siestas, evening strolls through squares of cooling fountains – may be at the heart of this serenity.

The river Tiber divides Rome. On the left bank are the original seven hills of ancient Rome and the modern city center, while on the right bank of the river is Trastevere, an

area of narrow streets leading into small courtyard-sized squares. In these tiny stone libraries of history, children may play football against a Renaissance pillared doorway, and washing may hang from a stone support taken from some once grand imperial palace. Ancient yesterdays survive side by side with modern reality.

Like other parts of Rome, Trastevere's streets are lined with family run *trattorie*, specializing in fish or pasta and vegetable dishes. Romans love to eat – there are some three thousand restaurants in Rome, as well as four thousand bars and pastry shops. They also love the cinema – Rome has over two thousand movie houses.

The Romans built baths on a huge scale – there was sufficient room for 1600 people in the Baths of Caracalla and 3000 at the Baths of Diocletian. These ruins would once have been the thriving focal point for social life; the elaborate system of aqueducts ensured a plentiful supply of water.

Right Rome is constantly rebuilt with fabric of the past. This alleyway probably contains stones trodden by the Romans, or quarried for Renaissance builders. However, the Romans, and their pets, treat this with insouciance.

Below In the Piazza Colonna is the Column of Marcus Aurelius, which was built in AD 174. Reliefs on the column depict battles and military maneuvers and the life of the times. The statue of the Emperor at the top was replaced with the figure of St Paul in 1589; the pedestal was added, and the base of the column restored, at the same time. It was owned by the monks of S. Silvestro, which accounts for its survival through the violence of the Middle Ages.

But perhaps the most important and lasting influences on Rome have been art and religion. The city is filled with magnificent art works, not only in galleries and museums, but on the streets. The Vatican is one of the world's greatest storehouses of western art treasures, while the paintings and sculptures of the great masters enrich many of the churches.

Napoleon described St Mark's Square in Venice as 'the drawing room of Europe'. Without a doubt St Peter's Square in Rome must be the drawing room of the world, with its superb Bernini columns embracing pilgrims from all over the globe. The Square is crammed with people on Wednesday and Sunday mornings, when the Pope gives the crowd his blessing and conducts multilingual services.

Rome can overwhelm the first-time visitor with the power of its history and the richness of its monumental treasures: where to start and what to see are questions difficult to answer. To survive as a visitor and to appreciate the city, it is perhaps best to take the centuries of history and art gently. Begin with a guided half day tour to familiarize yourself with your surroundings, then wander at will. Go sightseeing early or late to avoid the peak tour times at popular monuments. Get to the Vatican as soon as it opens and head straight for the Sistine Chapel, so that you can soak in its glory in relative seclusion (though talking is banned in the chapel). Wander the Forum late in the afternoon, and stop to refresh yourself at pavement cafés with a *granita al caffè* or a wonderful Italian ice cream.

At the end of a hard day's sightseeing, dine under the stars, sip a cool, light wine from the surrounding hills and listen to the strolling musicians. And don't forget to drop a coin in the Trevi fountain to ensure a speedy return visit to Rome.

Left Craftsmen are constantly engaged in restoration of the city, as ancient stones and timber are worn away by the pollution of the twentieth century. A skilled mason or carpenter can be sure of a lifetime's work ahead of him.

Below These two hurrying nuns seem oblivious to the somewhat disparaging look they are getting from above. In a city with so much statuary there will always be a cold stone eye watching from somewhere.

Right The Pantheon was originally a pagan temple for the Roman gods, but was consecrated as a church in AD 908. It has retained its appearance, except that instead of shrines to pagan gods there are Christian altars. The dome is as high as the diameter of the building and is lit by a single aperture at the top. It was covered with sheets of gilded bronze, but these were looted in AD 655 and replaced with lead.

Below Where the Corso Vittorio Emanuele is now there was once the 'Field of Mars' – an open plain used for military exercises and games such as chariot racing. The area fell into disuse when Witgis the Goth cut the aqueducts while besieging Rome in AD 537, and the people had to move nearer the Tiber to obtain water. All along the Corso Vittorio Emanuele ruins of Roman antiquities are juxtaposed with medieval cities and renaissance palaces.

Left Craftsmen are constantly engaged in restoration of the city, as ancient stones and timber are worn away by the pollution of the twentieth century. A skilled mason or carpenter can be sure of a lifetime's work ahead of him.

Below These two hurrying nuns seem oblivious to the somewhat disparaging look they are getting from above. In a city with so much statuary there will always be a cold stone eye watching from somewhere.

Right The Pantheon was originally a pagan temple for the Roman gods, but was consecrated as a church in AD 908. It has retained its appearance, except that instead of shrines to pagan gods there are Christian altars. The dome is as high as the diameter of the building and is lit by a single aperture at the top. It was covered with sheets of gilded bronze, but these were looted in AD 655 and replaced with lead.

Below Where the Corso Vittorio Emanuele is now there was once the 'Field of Mars' – an open plain used for military exercises and games such as chariot racing. The area fell into disuse when Witgis the Goth cut the aqueducts while besieging Rome in AD 537, and the people had to move nearer the Tiber to obtain water. All along the Corso Vittorio Emanuele ruins of Roman antiquities are juxtaposed with medieval cities and renaissance palaces.

Top The Piazza Venezia is probably the busiest, though by no means the most beautiful, square in the city. Due to the attentions of nineteenth-century town planners, it retains less of its Roman past than any of the other great squares. However, there are the remains of a first-century apartment building and a fragment of the tomb of C Publius Bibulus, which is of particular interest to historians as it is known to have stood at the beginning of the Via Flaminia, leading to the Adriatic.

Bottom An intimate view of a quiet street shows the characteristic color of the city which the visitor will carry away in the mind's eye. The emptiness of the street suggests that the afternoon siesta is well under way.

Right These two old ladies have possibly lived in close proximity to each other all their lives. They may well have stood together on a similar balcony as young girls and pretended not to notice the young men showing off in the street below.

Below The faces of these young men could well be found on the walls of one of the many art galleries. Caravaggio painted their like; only their clothes tell you which century they are in.

Top, facing page Anyone who likes Italian food will have developed a keen appreciation of antipasto. Here it is as its most tempting on home ground, with golden bread straight from a real Italian bakery.

Bottom, facing page One of the many joys of Rome is spending an evening at a lively, friendly restaurant. Here is the trattoria Meo Patacca, in Trastevere, settling down to a night of food and folksongs.

History and Legend

The Colosseum was officially named the Amphitheatre Flavium when it was inaugurated in AD 80. Part of its purpose was to provide spectacles for the general populace, who were becoming discontented by the way in which Emperor Nero had annexed a large part of the center of Rome for greater privacy. It was a sinister arena for violence and blood lust, where wholesale slaughter of wild animals, gladiators and Christians took place.

Until a few years ago, a caged she-wolf was kept on public display below the Tarpeian Rock, a modern-day reminder of the legendary wolf who suckled Romulus and Remus, the fabled founders of Rome. And a lasting memorial to the legend is on view in the Campidoglio Museum in the form of an Etruscan bronze. It is fitting perhaps that the twin sons of Mars, the god of war, are considered to be the founders of Rome, since much of Rome's history is checkered with wars and battles.

Rome was founded around 753 BC, strategically close to the sea, near the meeting of the lands of the Latins, Sabines and Etruscans. Some 240 years later the Romans revolted against the Etruscans and set up a republic that lasted over five hundred years. During this time the Romans created a powerful army which eventually gained control of the whole Italian peninsula and, after some hundred years of war, defeated Carthage in North Africa. The

fall of Carthage gave Rome control over the entire Mediterranean area, and her dominance spread far and fast – to Asia Minor, Syria, Palestine, Spain, France, the Rhineland and Britain. All came under the sway of the imperial eagles. Legions of soldiers marched out to their conquests along the six cobbled roads radiating from Rome and returned, victorious, along these same roads through triumphal arches, some of which still stand today.

Of course it didn't last. The rivalry between military commanders led to Julius Caesar's march on Rome in 49 BC. He ruled for five years, then was assassinated. Civil war broke out and the Republic fell apart.

Order was restored in 27 BC by Augustus Caesar and for 40 years Rome flourished, the center of a brilliant civilization. Architecture and the arts thrived; Horace, Ovid, Livy and Virgil were the writers of the day. And the Baths became the center of the

empire; at the Baths of Caracalla sixteen hundred people could bathe at the same time. The need of water for these baths encouraged the building of the aqueduct systems of Rome; in all 13 fed the baths, the longest four miles in length. A visible reminder of this massive civil construction – the Cloaca Maxima (great drain) – can be seen today in the Forum.

Roman law and language dominated the known world up until the third century AD in spite of the erratic temperaments and talents of the various emperors. Visible reminders of that power remain, such as the sweep from the Piazza Venezia down the Via dei Fori Imperiali to the Forum and the Colosseum.

Under the emperors, the seeds of Christianity flourished in spite of persecution – Peter and Paul preached amid the pagan deities which were worshipped in Rome. But many early Christians died fighting lions or gladiators in the 50 000-seat 'Flavian Amphitheatre', as the Colosseum was originally called. Built on the site of Nero's Golden House by 20 000 slaves, it still retains the grim memory of those bloodstained circuses in which thousands met their end. Much of the 1800-foot circumference was plundered of stone for later buildings, and in the thirteenth century it became a fort. In 1750, the pope declared the Colosseum sacred to martyred Christians and it is now said that when the Colosseum falls so too will Rome, followed by the rest of the world.

Though the fifth century saw the decline and fall of the Roman Empire, Rome survived the dark ages, with the attacks and sackings by various barbarian armies. Emperor Constantine converted to Christianity in the fourth century and the previously persecuted church of Rome emerged as the heroic leader. By the

Below A view of the interior of the Colosseum shows to some extent the daunting sight which must have met the eye of many a hapless victim as he entered the arena. Even the Vestal Virgins joined the eager crowds packed in the tiers of seats. However, those of particular sensitivity were allowed to sit in the upper levels, away from the smell of blood.

Left This magnificent Etruscan bronze she-wolf is in the Capitoline Museum. The twins Romulus and Remus were added in 1509 by Pollaiuolo. The legend is that they were the founders of Rome, and were suckled by a wolf; here she is seen defiantly keeping the world at bay while she nurtures her foster sons. This wonderful bronze is probably a fifth century work.

Below The Arch of Septimius Severus in the Forum was erected in AD 203 and has had a great influence on Western architecture, most notably seen in the Arc de Triomphe in Paris. It was built in honor of the emperor and his sons, celebrating their victories over the Parthians.

seventh century, the popes had taken over the rule of Rome. On Christmas Day AD 800, Pope Leo III crowned Charlemagne as emperor in St Peter's. A porphyry disc in the nave floor marks where the first Holy Roman Emperor knelt to receive his crown. And the empire survived until 1806.

Meanwhile the papacy went through a number of crises and changes; at one point the papacy was split and a second pope held sway in Avignon for 70 years. But the papacy returned to Rome in 1377 and the rebuilding of St Peter's began.

Although this period was turbulent, it was also the period when art and architecture blossomed under the patronage of the popes. Artists flocked to Rome to help rebuild, refurbish and redecorate under the flowering of the papacy. The building of St Peter's occupied much of the sixteenth century, and a testimonial to the richness of that time is the ceiling of the Sistine Chapel in the Vatican.

France conquered Rome in 1798 and made it a republic. Shortly afterwards Napoleon took the papal states as part of the French Empire, declaring Rome the second capital. After Napoleon's defeat, the pope was restored to Rome, along with all the art works removed during the Napoleonic wars, making the Vatican Museum one of the world's greatest collections of art.

Rome was declared the capital of united Italy in 1870 after the political struggles for Italian unification. The course of twentieth century Roman history is common knowledge: Italy suffered under fascist rule from 1922 to 1943, although in 1929 the Vatican became an independent sovereign state. After Mussolini's death and King Victor Emmanuel III's abdication, a republican constitution was set up under a president, with Rome, as always, the center of the country and of the government.

Facing page and below The visitor to the Forum today sees a bewildering mass of ruins, the result of much building and rebuilding over a long timespan – slightly less than a thousand years. The earliest remnants belong to 753 BC, and the Curia was built in the third century, giving a wide diversity of architecture. The ruins of the round temple of the Vestal Virgins are clearly recognizable, as are the arches of Septimius Severus and Titus. This would have been a center of the lives of the ancient Romans; religious ceremonies were held there, law courts gave judgments, gladiators met their deaths, and the ordinary people simply met to sell their wares or hear the latest news. It is at its most magical in the dusk, when most of the tourists have departed and silence falls.

Left Dominating this view of Rome is the Castel S. Angelo, its massive bulk looming over the Tiber. Once the mausoleum of Emperor Hadrian, it was extended and fortified in the Middle Ages and became a place of refuge for the popes in their struggles against anti-popes, imperialism and feudal barons. For many years during the Renaissance it was used as a prison and Roman families visit it to revel in its gory past somewhat as Londoners visit the Tower of London.

Below This scale model of ancient Rome is in the Museum of Roman Civilization. It is an excellent way of gaining a better impression of the relation of the buildings to each other, and the magnitude of the achievements of the architects who constructed the city.

Facing page The Piazza Bocca della Verità is one of the most picturesque spots in Rome. It is on the site of the old Forum Boarium, and here you can see the Temple of Vesta (so called because it resembles the Temple of the Vestal Virgins in the Roman Forum). Also in the square is the Temple of Fortuna Virilis, which was built around 100 BC.

Top, facing page The Quirinal Palace was begun in 1574 by Gregory XIII, and was intended as a summer residence for the popes. In fact, the Vatican had become such a center of intrigue and sinister doings that it was used as the papal residence until 1870. It then passed to the kings of Italy, and is now the home of the Italian president.

Bottom, facing page The building of the Farnese Palace began in 1514, but before long work was halted for lack of funds, and it was not finished until 1589; since that time there have been no additions. The top story is by Michelangelo, and there are two particularly beautiful salons, the Salon d'Hercule and the Gallery, which has a ceiling by Carracci which draws some inspiration from Michelangelo's ceiling in the Sistine Chapel. It is now the French Embassy.

Left The forbidding fortress of the Castel S. Angelo. In Puccini's opera *Tosca* the heroine leapt to her death from these battlements.

Below Tiber Island is quiet and secluded and still has many medieval buildings to stroll amongst.

Top, facing page In sharp contrast to ancient Rome, this stadium was built for the Olympic Games of 1960. It is in the EUR quarter, where many modern buildings were designed for Mussolini's international exhibition in 1940, which in fact never took place. However, the architectural style influenced much new building in other countries.

Bottom, facing page The Piazza Venezia is most notable for the monument to Vittorio Emanuele II. Its appearance caused British soldiers here in the war to call it 'the wedding cake'. Here it forms a dramatic backdrop to the policeman struggling to maintain order in the chaotic traffic flow

Below The urban sprawl of Rome always retains its charm, no matter how wild a configuration of periods, styles and materials the buildings may consist of. Romans are proud of their city, but regard it very much as a place to be lived in, rather than simply as a museum.

Ancient Architecture

This colonnade by Bernini flanks St Peter's Square, the columns standing four deep. Bernini designed and carried out the building of the whole piazza in only 12 years.

Rome could be described as one vast museum, where virtually every brick, piece of marble, or fragment of carving has evolved from older buildings, surviving fire, pillage and the ravages of time. The city has 58 museums and art galleries and 32 classified ancient monuments.

A noticeable characteristic of Rome's architecture is the wealth of obelisks and fountains. At one time there were 48 obelisks, brought from Egypt by the Roman emperors. Of these, only 13 now remain, the most notable being in the center of St Peter's Square. This is 84 ft high, and required the combined efforts of 900 men and 140 horses to raise it into place – a mammoth task that took four months.

Below The Sistine Chapel was built in the fifteenth century by Giovanni de' Dolci, and the walls were decorated by the greatest artists of the time, including Botticelli, Ghirlandaio and Pinturicchio. The side walls depict the life of Christ on one side and Moses on the other; the ceiling was originally painted in blue with gold stars, but Pope Julius II commissioned Michelangelo, whose Pietà he much admired, to decorate it. This task took Michelangelo four years, most of which he had to spend lying on his back as he depicted scenes from the Creation. Behind the altar can be seen his Last Judgment, painted some time later, in which is his self-portrait as St Bartholomew.

Right Beginning from the altar, the series of scenes in the center represent: the Separation of Light and Darkness, the Creation of the Sun and Moon, the Creation of Trees and Plants, the Creation of Adam, the Creation of Eve, the Fall and Expulsion from Paradise, the Sacrifice of Noah, the Flood and the Intoxication of Noah. On either side are prophets and sybils. This detail is the Creation of Adam – God stretches out his hand to touch life into the first man. In 1512, Michelangelo wrote to his father, "I have finished painting the chapel; the pope is very pleased with my work."

The skill of the Romans in constructing aqueducts ensured a plentiful supply of water from the surrounding hills, which was needed to feed the public baths and the numerous fountains, both focal points of the city's social life. Indeed, the fountains still provide a meeting place for families gathering in the evening to relax by the soothing sound of water splashing on stone. The greatest sculptor of fountains was Bernini, and Rome is adorned with testaments to his genius. Particularly beautiful is the Fountain of the Four Rivers in the Piazza Navona, which symbolises the Nile, Ganges, Danube and Rio de la Plata spurting from beneath an obelisk. In fact, in the time of the Emperor Domitian the stadium of the Piazza Navona was often completely flooded to provide an arena for mock naval battles and water sports. Two other fountains well worth a visit are to be found in the Piazza Barberini. These are the Triton, which has a figure blowing water from a conch shell, and the little Fountain of the Bees.

The most famous fountain, though, is the Trevi, which was the inspiration for the song 'Three Coins in a Fountain'. Commissioned by Pope Clement XII, it was completed by Salvi in 1762, and a legend soon grew that those drinking its pure waters would return to Rome. The water came from 13 miles away from an aqueduct built in 19 BC, and twenty million gallons a day run through the fountain. Today, visitors toss a coin in to wish for the luck of returning to Rome – these coins being collected later for charity, or simply by the local children.

Another legend surrounds the equestrian statue of Marcus Aurelius in Campidoglio Square. The statue was once covered in gold, and the legend goes that when it appears again in its former splendor the Day of Judgment will be heralded by a voice coming from the horse's forelock. Ancient Rome has also lost its gilding and much of the marble which once covered its palaces and temples. What remains is the original dark pinkish brick which now characterizes the ruins.

It is well worth going to see the scale model of Rome as it was in the time of the Emperor Constantine, which is housed in the quiet Museum of Roman Civilization at Eur. This gives a good overall impression of the splendor and might of the city in past times. Another place worth a visit is the Arch of Constantine, next to the Colosseum. The most intact arch left in the city, this is nevertheless a jigsaw puzzle of pieces of earlier arches.

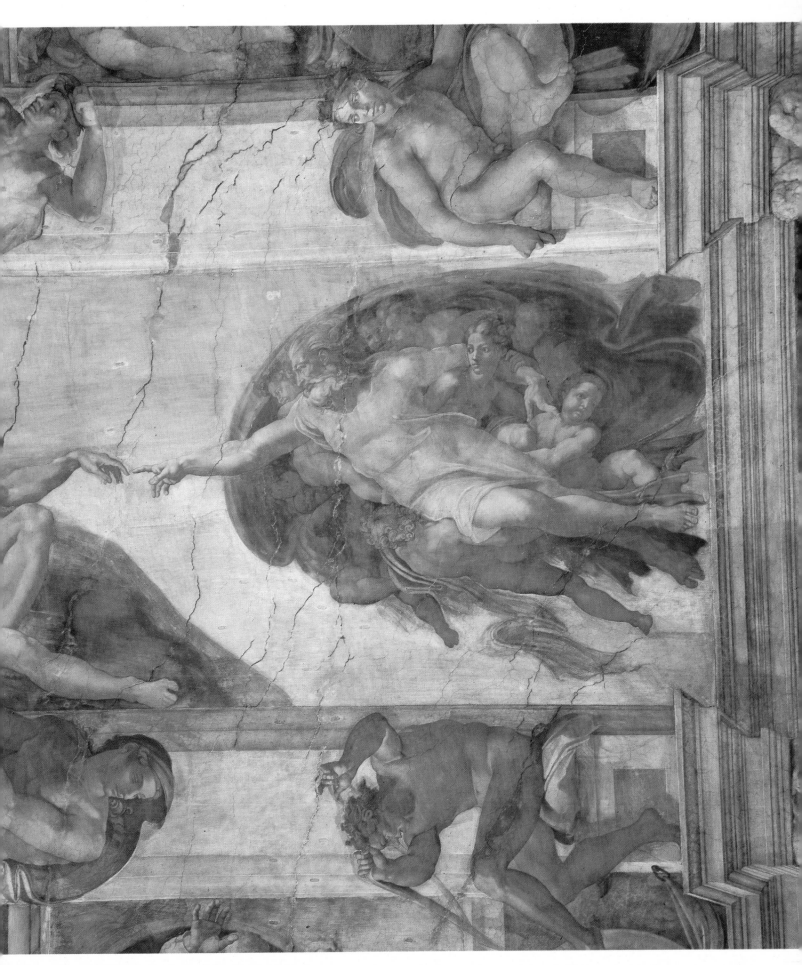

29

The Forum, which had been used from Renaissance times as a cattle pasture, was excavated through 20 ft of dirt in the nineteenth century. It is best to visit it early in the morning or at dusk when the noisy crowds have gone and the stealthy tribes of wild cats reclaim it. Strewn among the grass and shrubs are tawny stones, columns and pediments, marble floors and arches, and you will also find the remains of the circular temple of the Vestal Virgins who kept alive the perpetual flame – a ritual which had its origins in far distant times when fire was a precious thing to be carefully preserved. The ruin that remains today dates from AD 191, but there had been several earlier temples on the same site, all destroyed by fire.

Right In the Vatican is The Laocoön, which dates from the second century BC. It was discovered in 14 January 1506, and it was soon realized that it was the sculpture mentioned by Pliny. There is a recent rearrangement of the group next to a cast of what it was like for centuries, owing to erroneous restoration.

Below The Vatican is a labyrinthine complex of great halls and corridors containing the world's masterpieces of painting and sculpture. It is quite impossible to see everything in a single day; better to plan a selective tour and start early in the day before the crowds form.

Right In the basilica of St Peter's is Michelangelo's Pietà, the only sculpture that he ever signed. It was commissioned by the French Ambassador of the time, and the contract signed on 27 August 1498, stipulating that the work should be completed within one year. Michelangelo received some criticism for the youth and sweetness of the Virgin's face; but its charm and delicacy did not save it from being attacked in 1972 by someone with a hammer. Fortunately it has been restored by Vatican experts with such a high degree of skill that it is impossible to discern where the damage was. It is now protected by a toughened glass screen.

Other forums were created, among them Trajan's forum. Trajan's column, 138 ft tall, was raised in AD 113 and has survived almost unchanged. Reliefs covering the shaft represent the campaigns of Emperor Caesar Nerva Trajan Augustus and include some 2500 figures. The emperor's statue at the top was replaced by that of St Peter in the sixteenth century.

Not to be missed by the visitor is the Castel S. Angelo, which is also a favorite place for Roman family outings. Its thick, solid walls, with narrow places for boiling oil to be poured down on unwelcome intruders, show the city's need for strong protection after the collapse of the Roman empire. A dark and violent history as a fortress and state prison is reflected in its forbidding appearance, and immortalised in Puccini's opera *Tosca*, in which Tosca leapt to her death from the battlements.

After the sacking of Rome in 1527, a second beautiful city was created. The glories of Renaissance Rome are St Peter's and the Vatican Palace and its apartments. Pope Sixtus V (1585-90) was an apostolic architect who converted tangled medieval streets into straight avenues and completed the magnificent dome of St Peter's from which today one can have stunning views over the city. The church itself is the world's largest, covering three-and-a-half acres with 537 steps to its dome – the statues on its roof are 18 ft tall. St Peter's Square, designed in seventeenth-century baroque style by Bernini, is actually elliptical and took 10 years to design and 12 years to build. Its massive arena holds 300 000 pilgrims annually, gathered to hear the Pope's Easter blessing.

More great works of sixteenth-century architecture to see are Michelangelo's stairway in the Campidoglio, the Villa Medici, and the Quirinal Palace, now the home of the President of the Italian State.

Apart from in the Vatican Museum, sculpture from Roman times can be found in the National Roman Museum in the Baths of Diocletian and the Capitoline Museum in the Campidoglio. Here there are such treasures as the Dying Gaul, the Capitoline Venus and the Boy with the Thorn. The Capitoline Gallery has paintings by, among others, Caravaggio, Van Dyck, Velasquez, Titian, Tintoretto and Veronese, and paintings by Botticelli and Raphael and sculptures by Bernini can be seen in the Borghese Pavilion Gallery.

Right A view of the Spanish Steps, a famous rendezvous for people from all over the world. Beside them is the Keats-Shelley Memorial, a house where Keats once rented rooms.

32

Right This bronze statue of Marcus Aurelius in the Campidoglio was originally covered in gold.

Below and bottom Although the Capitol was once the center of Roman life, very little of antiquity remains. Michelangelo created two new façades for the existing palaces, and built a totally new one.

Monuments of more recent times are Mussolini's railway station and the EUR area, the 'Rome of Tomorrow'. This is the most modern section of Rome. Built in neoclassical style, it was originally intended for the Universal Exhibition in 1942 and although this was never held its designs influenced much subsequent building in the New World.

Rome is essentially a city where the citizens spend a great deal of time out of doors in the summer, walking, gossiping, eating and drinking. Consequently its many piazzas and steps complement its population. The most notable are the Piazza del Popolo, the Campidoglio and, nearby, the Piazza Venezia, with its monument to the first king of unified Italy, Victor Emmanuel II. Everyone, of course, has heard of the Spanish steps which lead from the Piazza di Spagna – their very name is synonymous with Rome. In April and May the staircase is banked with a mass of azaleas, and they provide a rendezvous for people from all over the world. The poet Keats once rented rooms by the steps and they are now preserved as the Keats-Shelley Memorial.

Left The Piazza Navona must be one of the finest of the large piazzas in the city. It is very popular at all times of the day, but particularly comes into its own at night, when the floodlights are illuminated and people gather at the pavement cafés. Bernini's Fountain of the Four Rivers provides a focal point; it was begun in 1648 at the behest of Pope Innocent X. The four figures at the base represent the four continents and their rivers; the Ganges (Asia), the River Plate (America), the Nile (Africa) and the Danube (Europe). They are accompanied by flora and fauna appropriate to the continent. On the top of the obelisk is a dove, which was the family emblem of the pope.

Left This delightful elephant, sculptured by Bernini, stands in the Piazza della Minerva. It was commissioned by Pope Alexander VII, who composed the inscription at the base. The theme of the elephant and obelisk is drawn from a fifteenth century romance, and it is ideally situated in this charming square.

Below In the Piazza Barberini are two Bernini fountains – the Triton, pictured here, and the Fountain of the Bees. The Triton dates from around 1637 and Bernini's use of travertine rather than marble was innovative, as was the realism of the figure. The square is one of the busiest crossroads of the city, which can make it difficult to gain a peaceful appreciation of these two beautiful fountains.

Right The Trevi Fountain is the most famous in Rome, being the one that inspired the song "Three Coins in a Fountain". It probably takes its name from the three streets – *tre vie* – that meet in the little square. The water that supplies it comes from Agrippa's aqueduct, which was built in 19 BC. The aqueduct was repaired in 1447 and a simple fountain placed in the square – the fountain that is there now was completed in 1762.

Right A detail from the Fountain of the Four Rivers shows the astonishing vigor and realism of the figures. In the building behind it, the Romans of today go about their daily life, taking this magnificent sculpture very much in their stride.

Below The whole wall of a palace is incorporated into the Trevi Fountain, filling nearly all of the little square. The fountain water has always been considered the best, softest and purest in Rome, which is probably why the legend arose last century that a traveler who drank it would return to Rome. At some point this was transmuted into a custom of dropping a coin into it. Charities and local urchins benefit handsomely from this.

Below The exterior of the Capitoline Museums should ideally be seen first at night to gain the full benefit of the theatrical atmosphere. Inside, you will find sculptures, paintings, coins and porcelain, some dating back to the time of Greek and Roman civilization, including the Capitoline Venus, the Dying Gaul and the Boy with a Thorn. Pictured here is the Empress Agrippina.

Right and bottom right Raphael is best known as a painter, but was also a sculptor of genius. His greatest works are to be found in Rome, in the galleries, museums and churches. The painting of The Lady with the Unicorn is to be found in the National Gallery of Ancient Art, and this fine sculpture is in the Borghese Gallery.

Right The Pinacoteca Museum in the Vatican is a separate building which was opened in 1932. It contains works by the greatest Italian masters – Giotto, Fra Angelico, Titian, Crivelli, Raphael and Caravaggio, the master of *chiaroscuro,* the contrast of light and shade. His "Deposition", pictured here, combines an awesome power with extreme delicacy, as seen in the curling tendrils of hair on the cheek of the sorrowing girl.

Art and Religion

4

The Pope is Bishop of Rome and also a sovereign in his own right as head of the Vatican State. One square mile in size, this State was founded in 1929 and contains St Peter's Church, St John Lateran Church, the Vatican and Castelgandolfo, the Pope's summer residence in the nearby Alban hills. There is an even smaller independent state – the Sovereign Military Order of Malta, which issues car registrations and passports from 68 Via Condotti!

The 'border' of the Vatican State is painted on the street at the edges of St Peter's Square. The population is under a thousand, but it has its own radio, railway station, newspaper, stamps and money. It even has its own guards – the Swiss Guards, wearing colorful uniforms reputedly designed by Raphael or Michelangelo. With the help of nuns, the guards check the clothes of visitors to ensure they do not offend their strict rules of decency and hawkers around St Peter's Square hire out plastic cover-ups for those who would otherwise be refused entry.

Just outside St Peter's is a good place to rest the horses and exchange some gossip. The drivers won't have to wait long for a hire in this favorite tourist spot.

The Vatican has a staggering total of a thousand rooms and contains museums and galleries of paintings, sculptures, the papal library (so big it has never been completely catalogued) the Borgia Apartments and the Raphael Rooms. The highlight of it must be the Sistine Chapel, with Michelangelo's ceiling. Michelangelo painted these scenes – depicting the Creation, the birth of Eve and the Fall – between 1508 and 1512, having to paint lying on his back on scaffolding. On the altar wall is his Last Judgment and the walls were decorated by other great artists of the time, including Ghirlandaio, Pinturicchio and Botticelli. When a new pope needs to be elected, cardinals are locked in this Chapel to vote. No contact is allowed with the outside world until a decision has been reached, so a signal smoke of burning ballot papers – white for a new pope, black to signify no decision – rises through a tall thin smoke stack from the chapel.

Protected by electronic security devices, the Vatican's 15 picture galleries house 460 of the world's greatest paintings. In addition, there are four rooms decorated by Raphael, and in the chapel of Nicholas V can be seen the work of Fra Angelico. In 12 cool rooms stand ancient sculptures, including the Laocoön and the Venus of Cnidus by

Left Some people spend their working lives in modern office buildings, others surrounded by sumptuous marble halls and art treasures. These two men of God, pacing the loggia by the Secretariat of State in the Vatican, would probably feel as bemused in a highrise apartment building as the tourist does when faced by the thousand rooms of the Vatican.

Right The Swiss Guards stand sentry at the entrance to the Vatican City. Their colorful uniforms were designed either by Raphael or Michelangelo. Although rules of dress have recently been somewhat relaxed, a strict sense of decency is still observed and those who wish to enter must pass muster under the watchful eye of the nuns and these guards. The unwary visitor will find plenty of hawkers nearby with plastic cover-ups on offer.

Below The square of St Peter's is a more familiar sight when packed with thousands of pilgrims awaiting the Pope's blessing. Nevertheless, in this picture it is easier to see the magnitude of Bernini's colonnades.

Praxiteles. The Vatican Library holds old manuscripts of the gospels, works by Virgil dating back 1600 years and, somewhat surprisingly, Henry VIII's love letters to Anne Boleyn. Etruscan gold jewellery, Egyptian mummies, Roman catacomb friezes, papal vestments and elaborate carriages can all be found within the Vatican walls. The Borgia family, of sinister repute, once lived in the Vatican's six Borgia Apartments.

St Peter's Church took 179 years to build, finally being consecrated in 1626. The high altar is a simple block of Greek marble from the Forum of Minerva, and only the Pope is allowed to celebrate mass there. It is canopied by a 95 ft high baldacchino designed by Bernini. Weighing 46 tons, it is made of metal stripped from the Pantheon, and is heavily encrusted with scrolls,

flowers and figures held up by barley sugar twist columns. In front of the 95 oil lamps burning before the alter is a sunken confessionale and bronze gates leading to the tomb of St Peter. Nearby, enclosed in a baroque sculpture by Bernini, is a chair believed to have belonged to St Peter and a bronze statue of him dating from the twelfth or thirteenth century, its toes worn thin by the kisses of the faithful. There is also Michelangelo's *Pietà*, the only sculpture he ever signed.

In all, there are five hundred churches in Rome and many contain priceless artistic and historic treasures. Some show how the many layers of Rome's diverse history became entwined – the Church of S. Clemente, near the Colosseum, has a twelfth-century ground floor and a Mithraic

temple to the sun god in its basement.

The Pantheon 'a temple to all gods', dates from 27 BC. It was reconstructed in its present form in AD 80 by Hadrian and became a Christian church in the seventh century. It is a circular building with a single magnificent dome for a roof lit by a circular opening in the dome. The 20 ton bronze doors remain, but much went to make St Peter's baldacchino and marble wall coverings have also been stripped off. Tombs to look for in the Pantheon are those of Raphael and the kings Victor Emmanuel II and Umberto I.

The church of S. Giovanni in Laterano (St John Lateran) has a religious art museum attached to it, and contains a wooden table upon which is believed that St Peter celebrated mass. It is the fifth church on the

Facing page The view from the dome of St Peter's is breathtaking. You can fully appreciate the magnificent symmetry of the Piazza and see far over the rest of the city. Stretching away from the Piazza is the contentious Via della Conciliazione, named after the conciliation between the Church and the State in 1929. It was begun in 1936, and many old houses, and in particular two streets, the Borgo Vecchio and the Borgo Nuovo, had to be pulled down to make way for it. However unpopular this may have been, it is hard to deny that traffic conditions in the area would have been untenable had they been left untouched.

Ancient and contemporary figures at St Peter's; *below,* stone figures atop Bernini's colonnade turn their cold gaze on the world, while *left* a cluster of undeniably human nuns smile at the camera.

site, the original dating from the fourth century. Opposite are the Scala Santa, the steps on which Christ was supposed to have walked in Pontius Pilate's palace in Jerusalem, and which were brought to Rome by St Helena. Roman Catholics ascend the steps on their knees.

St Peter is also associated with the church of S. Pietro in Carcere (St Peter in Prison), where, according to legend, Nero had him imprisoned. Before its consecration as a chapel, it was Tullianum prison and there is now an altar there with a relief depicting St Peter baptising his jailer.

St Paul too is much associated with Rome and is remembered by the church of S. Paolo fuori le Mura (St Paul's Outside the Walls). The original building was destroyed by fire in 1823 and the present church was built with the aid of donations from all over the world.

Near to St Paul's Gate is the peaceful Protestant cemetery where can be found the gravestones of Keats and Shelley. Again, paganism intertwines with Christianity with the huge pyramid tomb of Gaius Celestius dating from 12 BC to be found amongst the Protestant graves.

Left This view from the nave of St Peter's illustrates the extraordinary genius of the men over the ages who gave large parts of their lives to creating this supreme house of God.

Rome's oldest church is believed to be the gilded, mosaicked S. Maria in Trastevere, which dates from the third century. Legend says that a fountain of oil gushed from the ground on this spot on the day that Christ was born. Another particularly beautiful church dedicated to the Virgin Mary is S. Maria Maggiore, which has mosaic panels depicting scenes from the Old Testament and a main altar decorated with jasper, agate, amethyst and lapis lazuli. According to a fourth-century legend, snow once fell on the altar on 5 August, and accordingly white flower petals are showered on it from the dome on this date every year.

Right The Church of the Jesuits in the Piazza del Gesù was a place of prayer for the sculptor Bernini; he visited it every evening for the last 40 years of his life. There is much rich marble decoration, and the columns of St Ignatius of Loyola's tomb in the left transept are covered with lapis lazuli.

Below S. Maria Maggiore is one of the 'seven churches' of Rome which have always been a center for pilgrims. It was built in the fifth century by Sixtus III, and not, as is often thought, in the fourth by Pope St Liberius. Nevertheless, the vision that Liberius had of the Virgin telling to build a church where snow fell on 5 August is commemorated each year by a shower of white flower petals scattered on the altar.

Above In the church of S. Pietro in Vincoli is one of Michelangelo's greatest masterpieces, the sculpture of Moses on the tomb of Julius II. Placed here in 1544, long after the death of the pope, it is only a small part of the great monument Michelangelo had planned to put in St Peter's. Moses is depicted as he descends from Mount Sinai to find the Israelites worshipping the golden calf. The legend is that Michelangelo spent six months in the mountains looking for the right piece of marble for it; also that he once threw his hammer at the statue's knees, commanding it to speak.

Right Sixtus III built S. Pietro in Vincoli (St Peter in Chains) in the fifth century to house a relic of the chains in which St Peter had been bound in Jerusalem. Later, those which had bound him in Rome were added. The church is now so crowded with tourists who come mainly to see Michelangelo's Moses, seen here in its entirety on the tomb, and the relic of the chains in a bronze and crystal reliquary beneath the altar, that it is easy to overlook a fourth-century sarcophagus in the *confessio* behind the altar. This was not discovered until 1876.

Left S. Maria in Trastevere is one of the oldest churches in Rome, and is built on the spot where legend has it that a fountain of oil gushed forth when Christ was born. It was restored in the eighth century and rebuilt in the eleventh; it looks the same today as it would have done then. There is a beautiful mosaic on the façade of disputed date and more Byzantine mosaics of the Madonna inside. There is some doubt as to whether the ten female figures on either side of the Madonna on the façade represent the Wise and Foolish Virgins or not.

Below S. Clemente is a particularly interesting church. Below it is the Temple of Mithras, pictured here; above this Roman pagan temple are three successive Christian churches, built between the first and twelfth centuries. Although the church at first seems to be baroque, the visitor soon realizes that it has one of the most perfect medieval church interiors in the city. The earliest parts of the church date from before AD 385; the rest is fourth and twelfth century. There are some particularly beautiful paintings, including a Crucifixion attributed to Masaccio.

Facing page This astonishing *trompe l'oeil* ceiling is in the church of S. Ignazio. It represents the Entry of St Ignatius into Paradise and was painted by Andrea Pozzo: the best place to view it is from a small disc set into the pavement in the center of the nave. The decoration of the church throughout is very rich – there is a Baroque altar, and two lapis lazuli urns contain the relics of St Aloysius Gonzaga and St John Berchmans. The church was built between 1626 and 1685 by Andrea Pozzo and the architect Orazio Grassi, both of whom were priests.

Left The church of S. Carlo alle Quattro Fontane was a first commission for Borromini, who as a boy of 15 had been employed building St Peter's. He was an eccentric man, jealous of Bernini's success, who ultimately committed suicide; but this church was considered so excellent a work that Bernini recommended him to Pope Urban VII as the builder for the church of S. Ivo della Sapienza. The only light in S. Carlo alle Quattro Fontane comes from small windows in the dome, which are concealed by ornamentation, so the full effect of the *trompe d'oeil* decoration in the dome can only be seen on a bright day. It is decorated with octagonal, hexagonal and cross shapes which diminish towards the top, giving an effect of great height.

Hidden Rome

Escaping the 'people press' in Rome seems impossible, especially as you stand amid the traffic whirlpool in the Piazza Venezia, or weave your way between hooting, gesticulating drivers, and triple-parked cars. But there are gardens and tranquil places of retreat in Rome. It is soothing to sit under umbrella pines in the Borghese Gardens, Rome's largest piece of parkland, surrounded by marble statuary. You can wander, watch time pass on the water clock, picnic or doze in these gardens. Or you can stroll on the Janiculum hill where Garibaldi's forces fought a bloody battle. On its slopes is the North American college, a Roman Catholic seminary where American and Canadian priests are trained.

Little stone squares also provide a cool respite after a long day. The Largo Argentina near the Piazza Venezia holds the remains of four unidentified ancient Roman temples and has the more dubious honor of providing the home to Rome's largest stray cat community. Built in 1585, the Fountain of the Tortoises in the Piazza Mattei is a delightful oasis. Offbeat glimpses of the city can be had from the keyhole of the door to the private residence of the Grand Master of the Maltese Knights. Found in the Piazza dei Cavalieri di Malta, the view telescopes St

Peter's Dome one mile away in a most remarkable manner. Or, if you are energetic, climb the column of Marcus Aurelius in the Piazza Colonna for a rewarding view of the city.

Another of the charming legends of the city can be found in the Piazza Bocca della Verità, where a stone mask with a mouth received all the gossip and scandal of the centuries. It is said that the mouth will bite the hand of a liar.

Around the Piazza Navona, the Pantheon and Campo dei Fiori are narrow cobblestoned alleys, palaces, courtyards, fountains and old churches little visited by most tourists. And across the river is the Trastevere, full of twisting streets.

The dead of Rome make peaceful companions and the Protestant cemetery is not at all a sad place to meander. Living among tombs was indeed a way of life for early persecuted Christians in Rome. In times when it was forbidden to bury the dead inside the city walls, the catacombs were tunnelled out of volcanic stone by early Christians. They lived among the dead, sleeping on small stone bunks and living in narrow passageways. They wrote on the walls of these passageways, and you can see a note to St Peter and St Paul

Roman parks are a delightful mixture of fresh greenery and antique sculpture, fountains and pools. When the bustle of traffic and hooting of horns in the baking streets becomes oppressive, there is nothing nicer than to relax under the shade of a tree and rest the eye on cool white marble. Pictured here is the Temple of Aesculapius in the Borghese Gardens.

written by a man who had met them.

Although modern traffic may destroy some of the peace, a wander down the Appian Way is a passage back in time to the tombs of twenty generations. The ancient pavement, laid under Roman emperors, is preserved in many places and the road is lined with antique burial monuments framed by cypresses and umbrella pines.

Romans still flee the city, persecuted by its summer heat. Within a few miles of the city there are some delightful spots to visit, preferably midweek when most Romans are at work. Towards Tivoli lies Hadrian's Villa, certainly a must for any visitor to Rome. Hadrian built his private retirement villa with the help of some 20 000 slaves. More like a small city than a home, it has baths, temples, pools, statues and promenades. The Emperor's private living quarters are located on an island which is cut off from the rest of the complex by a swing bridge.

The Villa d'Este at Tivoli is another popular place – perhaps overpopular, since at least three bus tours a day visit the spot. But its terraced gardens, which overlook the plain back towards Rome, are cool and delightful. The fountains are in all shapes and sizes, organ pipes, jets and cascades – even an egg shaped one where you can walk under the overhang of water. Walk the right way round and it is said to bring good luck. To escape the crowds and souvenir stalls that line the way into the former cardinal's residence, walk up to the little-visited, but charming, Temple of Sybil on the hilltop.

Another escape can be made to the Castelli hills where the Pope retreats in summer to Castelgandolfo. The surrounding area is scattered with old villas, gardens, and restaurants in little towns. Here you will find towns like Frascati (of wine fame) and Grottaferrata, five miles from Castelgandolfo, which holds the Villa Fiorio.

Ostia is the port and seaside resort of Rome, and, while the beach is a sardine row of baking bodies, there are things to see. Look for the Scavi fish market with its mosaic pavements and the two thousand-

Right In the midst of the crush of people and traffic, a moment of peace as the generations meet by the water-tap much as they have always done over the centuries. The style of the traffic may have changed, but some aspects of Roman life continue very much as they have always been.

Below A different sort of view of Rome, but just as typical as the ornate churches and priceless works of art. Rome is not a stultified museum city, over-conscious of its rare and precious treasures; modern Romans live a busy life, dashing to work, growing plants on balconies, hanging out their washing. Someone who likes a modern, smartly painted home would recoil in horror at the thought of living in these flats; the Romans prefer mellowed stones.

year-old municipal buildings of the ruined town. The emperors tried to expand the City towards the sea gateway with little success, and Mussolini tried again in the 1940s, when he created EUR (Esposizione Universale di Roma). The neoclassical buildings are impressive; the Palace of Work with its arcaded ground floor lined with muscular statues is a good example of the style. Mainly residential and full of shady trees and parks, EUR is a little-known place for visitors to shop. The Via Europa offers a wide shaded avenue of shops containing leather goods and fashion accessories far cheaper than the main central shopping streets.

Left This fierce face is in the Piazza Bocca della Verità, which means 'the mouth of truth'. This is really a classical drain covering, and is in the portico of the church of S. Maria in Cosmedin. It was used in the Middle Ages as a kind of polygraph – the legend was that if anyone told a lie while holding their right hand in the open mouth the jaws would close.

Below The Fountain of the Four Tortoises is in the Piazza Mattei. This charming bronze fountain has a lightness and grace which is more characteristic of Florence, and indeed the sculptor, Taddeo Landini, was a Florentine. It was begun in 1581 and finished in 1584.

Facing page Hadrian's villa was the biggest and most sumptuous imperial villa in the Roman Empire. It was begun in AD 125 and took ten years to build – but Hadrian had little pleasure of it, since ill-health shortly afterwards forced him to move to a milder climate. Hadrian was a great traveler, and his villa shows influences from buildings in Greece and Egypt. Here, reproductions of statues found at the site stand among Corinthian columns on the edge of the Canopus, a stretch of water resembling a canal.

Left The Villa d'Este at Tivoli was planned in 1550, but so complex was the engineering for the fountains that they did not come into operation until the 1560s. Although the outside appearance of the palace is quite plain, the interior boasts sumptuous decoration and magnificent frescoes. You can take a special tour at night to see the beauty of the fountains and villa by floodlight.

Below Here the Tivoli Gardens can be seen in the context of the dramatic surrounding landscape.

Facing page The Protestant Cemetery is a peaceful and lovely place, with shrubs, lawns and flowers immaculately cared for. There is a walled garden in memory of Keats, who died in Rome of tuberculosis at the age of only 23. His tomb is nearby, with the words that Keats asked for on his deathbed inscribed: 'Here lies One Whose Name was writ in Water'.

Right The Via Appia Antica was completed in 312 BC by Appius Claudis the Censor. It runs dead straight to the Alban Hills, and was used for transporting armies and their supplies with all speed south and east. It is lined with pines, cypresses and pagan monuments marking the spot where Roman patrician families buried their dead.

Below Near the Via Appia are the Catacombs of St Calixtus. It used to be thought that the catacombs were used by Christians for practising their religion in secret, but scholars are now in general agreed that they were solely cemeteries. The galleries at St Calixtus would measure several hundred miles if they were laid out rather than being on different levels.

La Dolce Vita

Life for the average Roman citizen these days bears little resemblance to the film-created image of *la dolce vita* (the sweet life) of indolent rich jet-setters living their lives high and scandalously. A few minor jet-setters sit along the Via Veneto and in the Piazza del Popolo, gossiping and drinking coffee in the sidewalk cafés. For most people, life is family, work, shopping, eating and all the other preoccupations of ordinary life. Roman temperament, however, is reflected in the approach to the various crises which have beset the city, where dignity and elegance are still to be found.

Shade and siesta are sought and the pace slows dramatically for meals – lunch is at about three, and dinner starts at nine p.m. – and may last late and long. This is in ironic contrast to the frenzy of the traffic – the roller bowl of Vespas and other scooters weaving in and around a crush of cars, with the honking and hooting drivers, gesticulating traffic policemen and voluble political demonstrators adding to the general confusion.

Football is a Roman passion; when the city wins an important match, balconies blossom with swags of team colors, girls dress in the colors of the home team and Vespas trail banners of team ribbons. It's not surprising that 6500 police are needed to keep the Roman population in order during these celebrations.

Romans are sociable souls and mealtimes are very social occasions for most Roman families. Fresh fruit, vegetables, pasta, bread and meat are bought daily from neighborhood markets, bakers and pasta makers. People love to sit in cafés along the squares and courtyards, or, in the evenings, to stroll beside the cool, cascading fountains with their families.

Indolent when they can be, Romans are proud, cynical, indifferent to novelty or eccentricity. They love music and entertainment. During the summer there are concerts in the Basilica of Maxentius, and *son et lumière* in the Forum and the Tivoli gardens from early June to the end of September. The opera season starts in mid November and runs through to mid June, but there are summer performances held in the Baths of Caracalla, as well.

There are also numerous festivals, both religious and secular, throughout the year which draw massive crowds. Around Epiphany there is the Befana Festival in the Piazza Navona when the square is lined with booths selling sweets, toys and Christmas nativity figures. During the Easter period, on Good Friday, the Pope takes part in the Way of the Cross procession from the Colosseum to the Palatine Hills. Shortly after that, on 6 May, is the swearing-in of the new papal guard at the Vatican.

There are many more secular festivals. During the spring and fall, there are art fairs in the Via Margutta, while in July there is the Trastevere Expo with stalls of arts and crafts lining the banks of the Tiber. Food and wine are sold and there is music and fireworks. Following this festival is the Festa de Noiantri in Trastevere during the last two weeks in July. At the Festa, which is of pagan origins, the fun revolves around hefty feasting of Roman orgy proportions and lots of noisy games and music.

When lacking a religious or secular festival in the calendar, Romans like to go to the movies. A few decades ago Rome was considered the "Hollywood on the Tiber" because of its flourishing *Cinecittà* Studios and impressive film productions. Leading directors included Vittorio de Sica, Roberto Rossellini, Dino de Laurentis, Visconti, Fellini, Zeffirelli and, of course, Bertolucci.

As it is, there are still two thousand movie houses in the city, many showing dubbed American and other foreign films. Although films are fairly expensive, they are always packed until late into the night.

In high summer when the temperatures soar to around 95°F the people move out to the beaches and surrounding hills, leaving Rome to hardy visitors and the cat colonies. Romans go to the Tivoli gardens at night to stroll among the illuminated fountains and crowd the restaurants in the Alban Hills, the source of Rome's cooling waters.

Sundays are more peaceful in the city, when the roar of the traffic subsides, and the peal of church bells calling the faithful to mass ring through the ancient streets. Bells also herald in the New Year in Rome which is marked by quiet family dinners. One note at this point – be careful where you park your car on New Year's Eve; the populace greet the New Year by throwing their junk and old things out of the windows of their apartments and houses. It's a fine bargain-hunting ground for early risers.

Previous page Italians love their football. Here, the crowd give their all as Rome tackles Liverpool in the 1984 European Cup Final.

Facing page The visitor cannot help but take away a vivid memory of the mellow colors and solid arches of the Eternal City.

Right Imposing columns tower over a horse and driver, who take advantage of the shade they cast to indulge in a snooze.

Below In Rome, you can always find a stall selling something appealing. This old lady is solidly planted on the uneven cobbles, waiting for someone to buy a book or print.

Right In a bustling Roman market, a typically animated Italian conversation helps to pass the time in between bargaining with the customers.

Below Not a very convenient costume for chasing malefactors, this. However, these two carabinieri seem more interested in posing for the camera anyway.

Below right Roman markets sell delicious fresh produce, still smelling of the earth they grew in – no cellophane-wrapped frozen food here. And it has to be good quality; Italian women expect to pick out exactly what they want, so only the best gets by.

Chief among the pleasures Rome has to offer must be the wonderful shops which line its streets. The main streets for holiday shopping are perhaps Via Veneto and the Fifth Avenue of Rome, Via Condotti. Certainly one pays the price for the privilege of chic surroundings along these streets.

The headquarters of Gucci is in Via Condotti, as are Bulgari, Fiorucci, Valentino and Ferragamo. Leather, shoes, silks, fashion and jewellery of outstanding design and quality are there if you care to pay the price. Just off the Via Condotti, in the Via Borgognona, is a younger-style family fashion outlet run by a Gucci son. Here too, one can find the works of Missoni, the genius with knitwear.

Along the Via della Croce, look for sandals made to order, and good prices for gloves, bags, woollens, and shoes. This street, incidentally, is also well known for its delicatessens.

Antique hunters can browse in the Via dei Coronari, Via Giulia, and Via Babuino. For the penny pincher, seek out the more reasonably priced shops around the railway station like the Via Nazionale or Campo dei Fiori and Pantheon, or cross the Tiber to the secluded Via Cola di Rienzo and Via Ottaviano.

Every Sunday until 1 pm at the Porta Portese there is a traditional flea market with numerous bargains – from car parts to rugs and crafts. Not only is the market itself lively, there are strolling entertainers, fire eaters, gypsies and wandering minstrels. And behind the Basilica of St John Lateran is another market for clothes, North African silverware, crafts and leather goods. In the Campo dei Fiori every morning there are stalls of fruit, vegetables, cheeses, salamis and flowers.

The Via Veneto, leading from the Spanish Steps, is a mix of smart boutiques and cafés from which to watch the famous, rest and drink coffee after a long spell of shopping. 'People-watching' is quite fruitful in this area; certainly it is easy to tell who is the star of the moment, by the fuss and activity created by Rome's famous paparazzi photographers who specialize in the candid snap of the famous. The Via Veneto's fame is more hype than reality though, and native Romans prefer to sit in the cafés in the Piazza del Popolo.

Right However, cellophane wrapping is acceptable on some stalls. In the Porta Portese market, two Italian ladies appraise each other with, it seems, some degree of disapproval. The one on the stand appears to be getting the better of the encounter.

There are two Roman cafés that rank as monuments; the first is the Caffè Greco at 86 Via Condotti where a varied clientele have sipped and snacked. Luminaries like Goethe, Byron, Liszt, Buffalo Bill, Oscar Wilde and Tennyson have all at some point frequented this café. Appropriate busts and mementoes of the famous adorn the Greco's walls. The second of these famous cafes is the Babington Tea Rooms in the Piazza di Spagna where hot buttered toast, English scones and Nell Gwynn marmalade are served, an echo of the days when droves of English men and women made the Grand Tour.

Roman ice cream is a treat and most people agree that Giolitti in the Piazza del Pantheon serves the best. Some people however prefer Tre Scalini's iced confections in the Piazza Navona. Good coffee is available everywhere, and regardless of how you drink it – espresso, cappuccino or chilled as granita – it is a Roman bonus. If the day is chilly, there is no better way to start than with a pastry and a cup of frothy cappuccino sprinkled with cocoa.

Roman appetites are famous and the number of restaurants certainly bears this out. The range is enormous – from the ancient Ostaria dell'Orso to the simple *trattoria*, you will find something to fit any budget.

Rome is fortunately surrounded by wonderful farmland which produces the best fruit, vegetables and game one could want. And pasta, the staple of much Italian cooking, has been raised to an art form; *fettuccine Alfredo* has crossed the Atlantic from its native Rome. *Spaghetti alla carbonara*, with cream, beaten egg and bacon is another Roman favourite, along with *gnocchi alla Romana* and *stracciatella*, a clear soup into which eggs are beaten.

The ancient Romans gave the culinary world garlic, olive oil and wine, ideas they borrowed from the Greeks. Gastronomically, the world would be a

Left When in Rome, do as the Romans do . . . and take advantage of one of the many cafés where you can sit on the edge of a pretty street or square, contemplate a glass of grappa, and watch the world go by. This café is near the Spanish Steps; just right for a rest and a drink after walking up and down them!

Facing page, top The Tuscans have a special way of roasting meat on a spit – and this *girarosta toscana* will taste as good as it looks. In the foreground, a tempting display of fruit, olives, *prosciutto* and salami.

Right Italian men are renowned for their romantic treatment of the opposite sex – and it is never difficult to find a bunch of flowers. Conveniently sited in one of the most expensive and busiest streets, this stall no doubt does a roaring trade.

Below On the ground floor of a four-story building opposite Keats' house are Babington's Tea Rooms. As the name suggests, you will find a proper pot of tea here in the afternoon, but you can also lunch or dine here. The old-fashioned English flavor of the name is borne out inside, where the atmosphere is discreet and dignified and the service efficient and courteous. It has hardly changed since it was opened 80 years ago.

poorer place without these contributions.

On the whole, Roman cuisine is of the homey sort, rather than ultra elaborate or rich. It is based on a few good ingredients. Raw vegetables and salamis may start a meal – artichokes cooked in olive oil are a great seasonal favourite. For meat courses, there is roast suckling lamb from the salt marshes nearby, oxtail stewed with herbs and wine, chicken with sweet peppers, boar with sweet and sour sauce, roast suckling pig perhaps or *saltimbocca alla Romana* – a veal fillet with ham and sage cooked in butter with a white wine sauce.

For dessert most Romans take fruit or macedonia fruit cup, but there are more elaborate concoctions like *zuppa inglese*, "English soup", which bears more than a passing resemblance to trifle.

And along with the meal, the little family run restaurants serve *bruschetta*, a home-baked bread toasted, rubbed with garlic, olive oil, salt and pepper.

Cheeses, too, are used in Roman cooking. Mozzarella, the buffalo milk cheese of the south, is much used, as is soft ricotta, made from ewe's milk. And wine. No meal is complete without Castelli Romani wines from the Alban hills; Frascati is one of the best known.

When the temperatures soar in the summertime, the city moves out to the country inns along the Via Cassia and Via Flaminia where tables groan under the weight of antipasti and grilled meats.

RADIO TAXI
TEL. 3570
MONZA

Facing page, top A phalanx of Roman faces at the Colosseum. The expression on the face of the nun implies she can imagine all too clearly the bloody scenes that were enacted there centuries ago – being a Christian was indeed a precarious way of life then.

Facing page, bottom This taxi driver looks a bit bored, but he will soon leap into action when a passenger gets in. Roman taxi drivers will take you anywhere you want to go – but expect to take the corners fast and remember that you don't actually *need* all four wheels on the road at once . . .

This page, top You might think the headgear looks a trifle strange with the sunglasses, but Palm Sunday doesn't have to be observed with undue solemnity. Religion is very much a part of life here, and there is no need to adopt a reverent stance to show you are a true Catholic.

This page, center People come from all over the world to Rome for Palm Sunday, bearing aloft their banners to show their home base. Rome is the very center of the Catholic religion, and all of these people will try to get into St Peter's Square to receive the Pope's Easter blessing.

This page, bottom Football is almost a religion, too. An Italian crowd will give the visiting team a hard time, and these Liverpool players can expect some hefty booing if they score a goal.

Major Attractions

1 St Peter's Basilica, Square and the Vatican City. The Vatican is a state governed by the Pope, and is surrounded by a wall built to protect St Peter's tomb. St Peter's Square is familiar to millions as it is seen packed with pilgrims to receive the Pope's Easter blessing. Don't miss Michelangelo's ceiling in the Sistine Chapel, one of the wonders of the world.

2 The Forum. Originally designed as the center of social, judicial and political life of ancient Rome, it has few buildings left standing. However, you will be able to recognize the Arches of Titus and Septimius Severus and the Temple of the Vestal Virgins.

3 The Colosseum. Built for a grim purpose, the Colosseum still retains a sinister feel. Here thousands of Christians were fed to the lions and gladiators engaged in fights to the death under the appreciative gaze of the emperors and citizens of Rome.

4 Castel Sant' Angelo. This fortress was built over Hadrian's mausoleum and became both a refuge for the popes in their battles against feudal barons and anti-popes, and a political prison. Stories of torture and murder are attached to it.

5 Villa Borghese. Rome's largest public park, it was laid out at the beginning of the seventeenth century and became a public park in 1902. There is a lake, where one can take a boat, entertainments in the Piazza di Siena, and plenty of statuary to see.

6 Piazza Venezia. Chiefly notable for the monument to King Vittorio Emanuele II, this square is a place to keep a weather eye on the traffic, which seems to obey no rules at all! The monument has been nicknamed "the wedding cake" because of its appearance.

7 Piazza Navona. In the center of this square is Bernini's Fountain of the Rivers. A market of sweets and toys is held here before Epiphany.

8 Piazza di Spagna. This is one of the most romantic squares in the city. Leading off it are the Spanish Steps, which provide a rendezvous for people from all over the world. Next to them is the Keats-Shelley Memorial, the house where the poets Keats once rented rooms.

9 St John Lateran. This church was originally built in the fourth century, was destroyed by vandals and restored in the fifth. An earthquake ruined it in the eighth century and it was rebuilt in the ninth; in the fourteenth century it was twice burnt down! Consequently, what you can see today has little of the original remaining. In 1932 some 23 architects competed to design the facade it still has today.

10 The Quirinal Palace. For a while this was the residence of the popes, but then it passed to the kings of Italy. It is now the home of the Italian President.

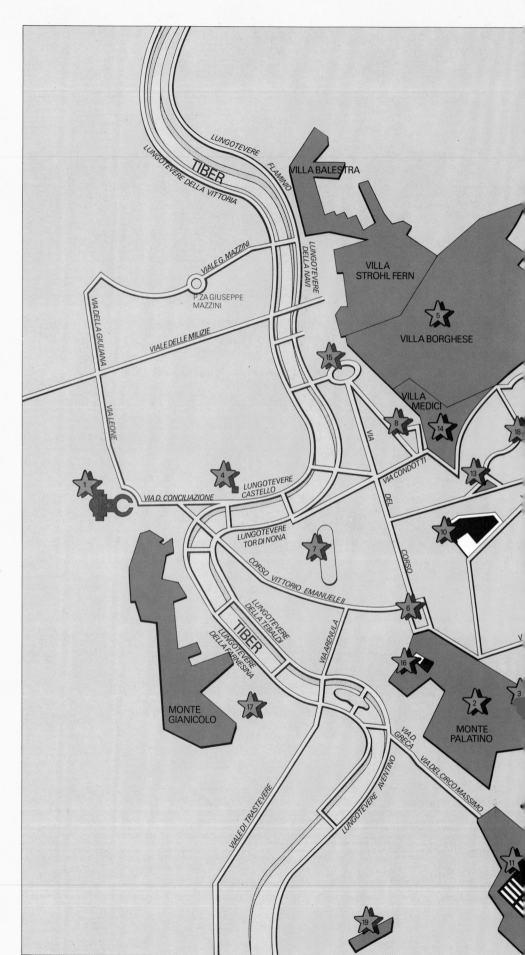

Facing page, top A phalanx of Roman faces at the Colosseum. The expression on the face of the nun implies she can imagine all too clearly the bloody scenes that were enacted there centuries ago – being a Christian was indeed a precarious way of life then.

Facing page, bottom This taxi driver looks a bit bored, but he will soon leap into action when a passenger gets in. Roman taxi drivers will take you anywhere you want to go – but expect to take the corners fast and remember that you don't actually *need* all four wheels on the road at once . . .

This page, top You might think the headgear looks a trifle strange with the sunglasses, but Palm Sunday doesn't have to be observed with undue solemnity. Religion is very much a part of life here, and there is no need to adopt a reverent stance to show you are a true Catholic.

This page, center People come from all over the world to Rome for Palm Sunday, bearing aloft their banners to show their home base. Rome is the very center of the Catholic religion, and all of these people will try to get into St Peter's Square to receive the Pope's Easter blessing.

This page, bottom Football is almost a religion, too. An Italian crowd will give the visiting team a hard time, and these Liverpool players can expect some hefty booing if they score a goal.

Major Attractions

1 St Peter's Basilica, Square and the Vatican City. The Vatican is a state governed by the Pope, and is surrounded by a wall built to protect St Peter's tomb. St Peter's Square is familiar to millions as it is seen packed with pilgrims to receive the Pope's Easter blessing. Don't miss Michelangelo's ceiling in the Sistine Chapel, one of the wonders of the world.

2 The Forum. Originally designed as the center of social, judicial and political life of ancient Rome, it has few buildings left standing. However, you will be able to recognize the Arches of Titus and Septimius Severus and the Temple of the Vestal Virgins.

3 The Colosseum. Built for a grim purpose, the Colosseum still retains a sinister feel. Here thousands of Christians were fed to the lions and gladiators engaged in fights to the death under the appreciative gaze of the emperors and citizens of Rome.

4 Castel Sant' Angelo. This fortress was built over Hadrian's mausoleum and became both a refuge for the popes in their battles against feudal barons and anti-popes, and a political prison. Stories of torture and murder are attached to it.

5 Villa Borghese. Rome's largest public park, it was laid out at the beginning of the seventeenth century and became a public park in 1902. There is a lake, where one can take a boat, entertainments in the Piazza di Siena, and plenty of statuary to see.

6 Piazza Venezia. Chiefly notable for the monument to King Vittorio Emanuele II, this square is a place to keep a weather eye on the traffic, which seems to obey no rules at all! The monument has been nicknamed "the wedding cake" because of its appearance.

7 Piazza Navona. In the center of this square is Bernini's Fountain of the Rivers. A market of sweets and toys is held here before Epiphany.

8 Piazza di Spagna. This is one of the most romantic squares in the city. Leading off it are the Spanish Steps, which provide a rendezvous for people from all over the world. Next to them is the Keats-Shelley Memorial, the house where the poets Keats once rented rooms.

9 St John Lateran. This church was originally built in the fourth century, was destroyed by vandals and restored in the fifth. An earthquake ruined it in the eighth century and it was rebuilt in the ninth; in the fourteenth century it was twice burnt down! Consequently, what you can see today has little of the original remaining. In 1932 some 23 architects competed to design the facade it still has today.

10 The Quirinal Palace. For a while this was the residence of the popes, but then it passed to the kings of Italy. It is now the home of the Italian President.

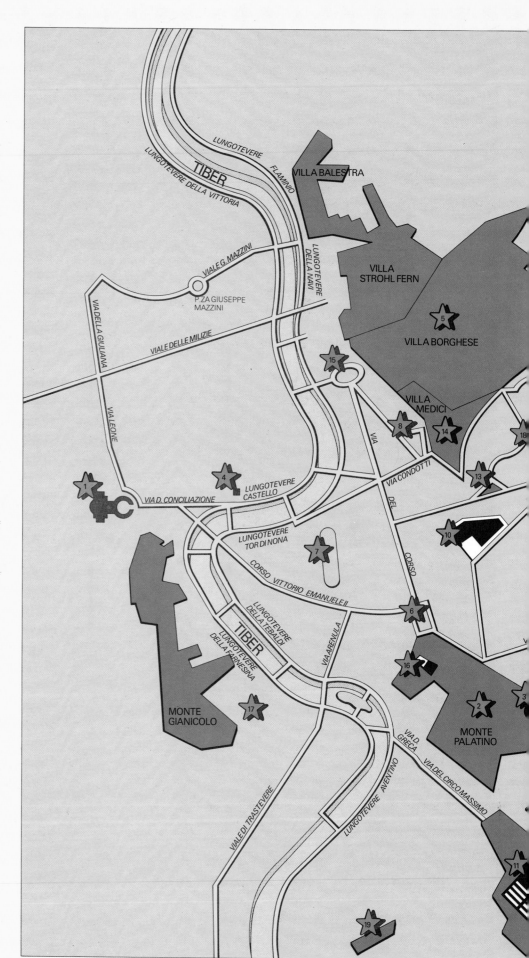

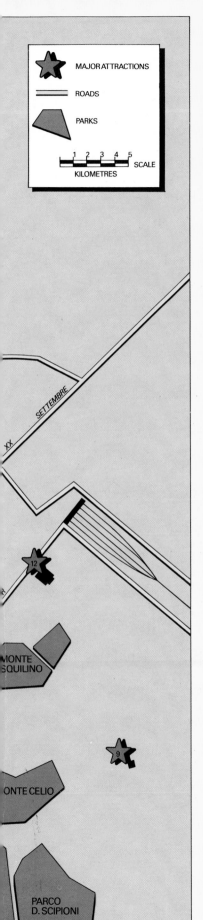

11 The Baths of Caracalla. These were begun by Septimius Severus in AD 206. They were able to accommodate 1600 people at once, and were used until the sixth century, when the Goths destroyed the aqueducts which supplied their water.

12 Santa Maria Maggiore. Legend says that on this spot a fall of snow once occurred on 5 August. Accordingly, white flower petals are sprinkled on the altar on this date every year. There are mosaics and a triumphal arch inside which date from the fifth century.

13 Piazza Barberini. This is a pivotal part of the city, which means that it is hard to take a peaceful look at Bernini's Triton Fountain. However, it is worth persevering, since the fountain, with its four dolphins and Triton, is particularly delightful.

14 The Villa Medici. Galileo was once imprisoned here by order of the Inquisition. The fountain in front of it once had a Florentine lily in it; the cannonball you will see there today was put there after Queen Christina of Sweden fired one of the cannons at the Castel Sant' Angelo with more enthusiasm than accuracy and hit the Villa Medici instead of the heavens!

15 Piazza del Popolo. This square has three especially beautiful churches – Santa Maria in Montesanto, Santa Maria dei Miracoli and Santa Maria del Popolo. The latter contains paintings by Caravaggio.

16 The Campidoglio. Here you will find magnificent classical sculptures in the Capitoline museums, a statue of Marcus Aurelius, and facades by Michelangelo. The Capitoline Hill served as a fortress in early times, and the Capitoline Temple of Jupiter was the center of Roman religious life.

17 Trastevere. To see the best side of Trastevere go after dark, when the restaurants start to buzz with life and atmosphere. The Trasteverini think they are of purer Roman stock than their counterparts across the river, many of whom only arrived after 1870! It is now much smarter than formerly, but there are still *trattorie* that offer food that is both wonderful and cheap.

18 Via Veneto. This is one of the smartest streets in town, where you can expect to see famous faces. There are two cafes, Doney's and the Café de Paris, which have a cosmopolitan clientele, the former attracting mainly Americans.

19 The Protestant Cemetery. This charming, peaceful place is delightful to wander in on a hot day when the city's bustle becomes overbearing. Here you will find the grave of Keats, and Trelawney buried Shelley's heart in this cemetery.

PICTURE CREDITS